Catherine

Best wishes

Rob Kesseler

2009

PUBLISHED BY
THE WORDSWORTH TRUST AND GRIZEDALE ARTS

FIRST PUBLISHED IN 2001 BY THE
ROB KESSELER, GRIZEDALE ARTS AND THE WORDSWORTH TRUST

BRITISH LIBRARY CATALOGUING-IN-PUBLICATION DATA:
A CATALOGUE RECORD FOR THIS BOOK IS AVAILABLE AT THE BRITISH LIBRARY.

ISBN 0 9525450 3 9

GRIZEDALE   THE WORDSWORTH TRUST
AMBLESIDE   DOVE COTTAGE
CUMBRIA   GRASMERE
LA22 8QJ   CUMBRIA LA22 9SH

www.grizedale.org   www.wordsworth.org.uk

RUSKIN TEXTS REPRODUCED BY KIND PERMISSION FROM
THE RUSKIN FOUNDATION (RUSKIN LIBRARY, UNIVERSITY OF LANCASTER).
MAPS REPRODUCED BY KIND PERMISSION OF THE FORESTRY COMMISSION.

DESIGN STUDIO TONNE, DESIGN@TONNE.ORG.UK
PRINTED IN THE UK BY GEOFF NEAL LITHO, MIDDLESEX

WITH VERY SPECIAL THANKS TO: DR. MADELINE HARLEY,
ADAM SUTHERLAND, ROBERT WOOF, PAMELA WOOF, ROBERT HEWISON,
SIMON STEVENS, AGALIS MANESSI, PAUL FARLEY, PAUL FARRINGTON.

FINANCIAL ASSISTANCE FROM GRIZEDALE, THE WORDSWORTH TRUST,
NORTHERN ARTS, THE ARTS COUNCIL OF ENGLAND, THE LONDON INSTITUTE,
CENTRAL SAINT MARTINS COLLEGE OF ART & DESIGN, REGIONAL ARTS LOTTERY PROGRAMME.

  THE LONDON INSTITUTE

WITH SUPPORT FROM JOSIAH WEDGWOOD & SONS LTD

WEDGWOOD

POLLINATE

ENCOUNTERS WITH LAKELAND FLOWERS

ROB KESSELER

A POLLEN CALENDAR

PAUL FARLEY

*

Wordsworth wouldn't know
these syllabic off-comers.
Japan still tight closed.

*

Watching the birds eat
the coconut, seed and fat
while observing Lent.

*

A junk mail promise
to help my home finances
blossom: straight in bin.

*

Hear the Manx mail plane?
The Doppler of half-past-twelve
crop-dusting my dreams.

*

Million, billi-
on, trillion, quadrilli-
on: the pollen count.

*

Summer's circulars:
cornflower, forget-me-not
on a hiker's boot.

*

'Carefully remove
any dust from your Nikon's
lens with some dry lint.'

*

A walk round the lake
the night of the Perseids'
split second annuals.

*

The geese in fives
and sevens: sales of anti-
histamines falling.

*

Resident poet
given free board to ponder
his propaganda.

*

Two business cards
from an Ambleside plumber
on my mat: first frost.

*

Took this saijiki
up Silver How in the snow
with a flask of tea.

CONTENTS

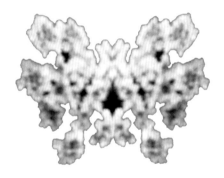

FOREWORD

ADAM SUTHERLAND
DIRECTOR, GRIZEDALE
ROBERT WOOF
DIRECTOR, THE WORDSWORTH TRUST

This book is the culmination of a project that began as a collaboration between Rob Kesseler and Grizedale and has been published to coincide with an exhibition for the Wordsworth Trust. Bringing together the worlds of science and art the artist set out to examine and celebrate Lakeland flora as observed through a Scanning Electron Microscope and the writings of John Ruskin and Dorothy and William Wordsworth.

Pollination is a mysterious and magical event, and pollen grains or 'magic bullets' as Richard Dawkins likes to call them, complex and fascinating forms. Cross fertilisation requires a timely concurrence of circumstance, and, as it is with flowers, so it is with art. From what began as a chance idea on an unexpected walk through Grizedale Forest, has blossomed into a whole series of works that exploit the decorative potential of this unseen world at our feet. Pollinate weaves together the rich collection of images and words that working in the Lakes has inspired.

FLORID

From an early age my encounters with flowers provided me with a curious mixture of experiences that clearly set the seeds for a hybridised approach to floral material. Firstly there was my father's aunt who regularly filled her house with plastic flowers. As they became faded and dusty they were planted out in the garden in the flowerbeds, where over several years they gradually replaced the few plants that had grown naturally. Tulips, daffodils, lupins, roses, chrysanthemums, and dahlias formed a polychrome border, resistant to all weathers and in bloom throughout the year.

Then there was my mother who liked to take me to the Women's Institute flower arranging class, where at the age of thirteen and with a burgeoning and anarchic desire to test out the artistic limits of this medium, I attempted to contort flowers and scrap metal into an unnatural alliance, a new botanical brutalism.

Being an engineer with more of an interest in how things work as against what they look like and perhaps to provide an element of balance in my botanical education, my father gave me an old and very beautiful brass microscope. This revealed a new world of colour and structure and one that had to wait nearly forty years to bare fruit .

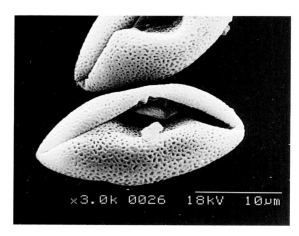

Narthecium ossifragum
Bog asphodel
SEM   x3000

among the woods

Following these florid influences, many years have subsequently been spent exploring the ways in which botanical imagery has been used within the decorative arts and the way in which flowers have been manipulated to conform to accepted notions of natural beauty. In 1998 on a visit to the Lake District, I passed through Grizedale Forest and was struck by the possibility of producing a work that used the materials from the forest in a new way. I wanted to create a work that originated from that place but was unlike anything else there.

I was aware that others had been there before me.

Monday 9th.

In the morning William cut down the winter cherry tree
I sowed French Beans & weeded. A coronetted Landau
went by when we were sitting upon the sodden wall.
The ladies (evidently Tourists) turned an eye of interest
upon our little garden & cottage.

Dorothy Wordsworth,Grasmere Journal, June 1800

These Tourists, Heaven preserve us! needs must live
A profitable life: some glance along,
Rapid and gay, as if the earth were air,
And they were butterflies to wheel about
Long as their summer lasted; some as wise,
Upon the forehead of a jutting crag
Sit perched with book and pencil on their knee,
And look and scribble, scribble on and look,

The Brothers, William Wordsworth, 1800

As the two extracts from Dorothy and William Wordsworth demonstrate the consumption of the natural beauty of the Lake District was well under way at the end of the 18th century. Already earlier in the century the Grand Tour had fostered an appreciation of landscape that elevated gardening to a status equal to that of painting and poetry, heralding the development of the English landscape garden carefully arranged and ordered into classical and pastoral vistas.

It is not surprising therefore that this passion was exploited by the burgeoning manufacturing industries, spawning a veritable cornucopia of decorative objects for the home. At the forefront of this wave was the master potter and entrepreneur Josiah Wedgwood, whose commission from Catherine the Great of Russia in 1773 culminated in a remarkable 952 piece dinner service individually decorated with images of the British Isles based on drawings and engravings made by contemporary artists. Initially views of the homes and gardens of the nobility, the choice of subjects was extended to include romantic scenes of the industrial revolution and views of the wilder and more remote parts of Wales, Scotland and the Lakes. In this way Wedgwood exported a powerful visual statement of Britain that spoke of beauty, power and wealth.

Dessert plate decorated with a view of Aysgarth Bridge, North Yorks. c1774 Wedgwood Museum, Barlaston, Staffs.

Flora Danica, Dish for custard cup - Thorn Apple,
c1780-1800, The Royal Silver Room,
Christiansborg Palace, Denmark.

The botanical sciences were also going through a period of rapid expansion, and in 1790 at what was later to become the Royal Copenhagen Porcelain factory, a project even more ambitious in scale than Wedgwood's was commenced. 'Flora Danica', inspired by the botanical reference book of the same name comprised of over 1800 individual items of tableware each decorated with painstaking accuracy with a plant illustration from the book. Drawing upon the work of Georg Christian Oeder, physician, botanist, economist, professor and advisor to the royal court it recognised the scientific, economic and political value that the study of plants could have to a trading nation.

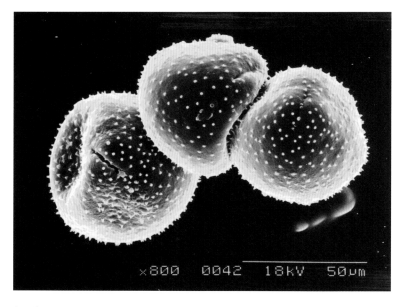

Lonicera
Honeysuckle
SEM   x800

Inspired by these two great dinner services I set out to create a work that extended this tradition developing new floral imagery through the use of contemporary botanical science. Recalling my brass microscope, the potential to work with material invisible to the naked eye was appealing, to reveal and to celebrate a small part of the forest.
The material chosen was pollen, a fertile germinator rich in form and metaphor, which when viewed under a scanning electron microscope at magnifications of up to x5K reveals highly individual and complex structures.

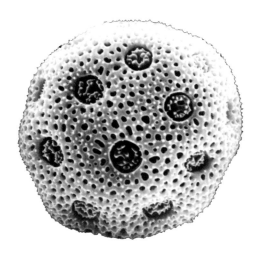

The study of pollen is not new. As early as 1676 in his book, 'The Anatomy of Flowers, prosecuted with the bare eye, and with the Microscope', Nehemiah Grew describes in accurate detail the forms and functions of pollen from different plants. In the 1830's the German botanist Carl von Fritzsche produced a collection of drawings classifying pollen forms that anticipated the later Victorian predilection for turning nature into ornamental form.

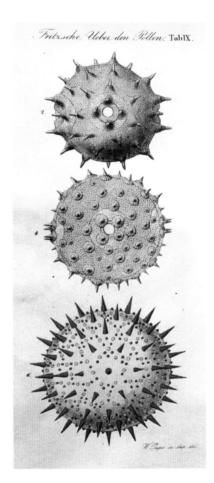

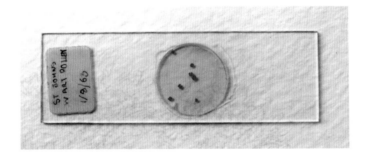

Microscope slide of St John's wort pollen,
Rob Kesseler, 1963.

Carl von Fritzsche, 1833.
Drawings for pollen classification.
Royal Botanic Gardens, Kew.

Nehemiah Grew, Anatomy of Flowers prosecuted with the
bare eye and with the microscope, 1682. Royal Botanic Gardens, Kew.

f.12.
The Attire (e)
in f. 11.

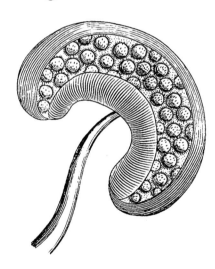

f.13.
Ine of ỹ Thecæ (t)
in f.12.

6. §.   And as the young and early *Attire* before it opens, answers to the *Menses* in the *Femal :* so is it probable, that afterward when it opens or cracks, it performs the *Office* of the *Male.* This is hinted from the *Shape* of the *Parts.*   For in the *Florid Attire,* the *Blade* doth not unaptly resemble a small *Penis,* with the *Sheath* upon it, as its *Præputium.*   And in the *Seed-like Attire,* the several *Thecæ,* are like so many little *Testicles.*   And the *Globulets* and other small *Particles* upon the *Blade* or *Penis,* and in the *Thecæ,* are as the *Vegetable Sperme.*   Which, so soon as the *Penis* is exerted, or the *Testicles* come to break, falls down upon the *Seed-Case* or *Womb,* and so Touches it with a *Prolifick* Virtue.

f. 14.
The *spermatick Globulets* in *f. 13.*

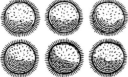

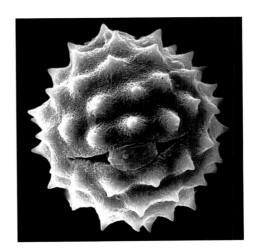

Towards the end of the seventeenth century
the study of plants was also becoming an
acceptable pastime, and in her journal for the
16th May 1800 Dorothy Wordsworth proclaimed,

"Oh! that we had a book of botany –
all flowers now are gay and deliciously sweet."

A year later William had acquired a botanical
microscope and two copies of William Withering's,

'Arrangement of British Plants according to the
latest Improvements of the Linnean System and
an Introduction to the Study of Botany.'

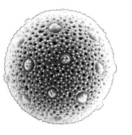

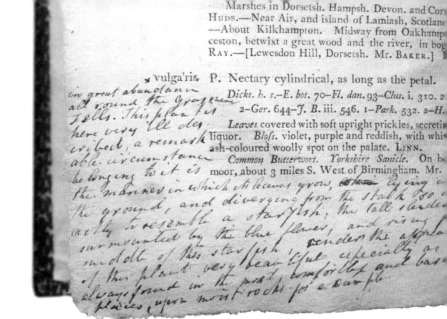

William Withering, Arrangement
of British plants according to the
latest improvements in the Linnean
System and an introduction to the
Study of Botany.

Marginalia, William Wordsworth.
The Wordsworth Trust.

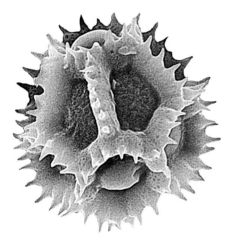

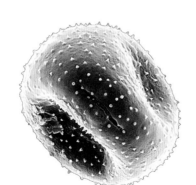

In an age of environmental conciousness, the youthful innocence of picking wild flowers is but a fleeting moment that swiftly moves from the magical discovery of natures splendours to an apparent act of vandalism. This urge to pluck and the awareness of a need for restraint pull in opposite directions.

"And often, trifling with a privilege
Alike indulged to all, we paused, one
now, And now the other, to point out,
perchance to pluck, some flower or
water - weed, too fair either to be
divided from the place on which it grew,
or to be left alone to its own beauty".

William Wordsworth, Poems
on the naming of places IV, 1799.

For Dorothy Wordsworth the urge proved too great and her conscience was quickly pricked.

"I found a strawberry blossom in a
rock, the little slender flower had more
courage than the green leaves, for they
were but half expanded and half grown,
but the blossom was full spread out.
I uprooted it rashly, and I felt as though
as I had been committing an outrage,
so I planted it again - it will have but a
stormy life of it, but let it live if it can".

Dorothy Wordsworth,
Grasmere Journal, 31st January 1802

With the development of the project, my desire to pick with a clear conscience was satisfied, and over several visits I collected pollen from flowers and plants in Grizedale Forest, Brantwood House, John Ruskin's home on the shores of Lake Conniston and from Dove Cottage at Grasmere, home to William and Dorothy Wordsworth. These pollen samples were photographed on a Scanning Electron Microscope at Kew Gardens and the resulting images used to develop a collection of burnished gold and enamel ceramic prints that were used to decorate a dinner service for Grizedale and a tea set for Dove Cottage.

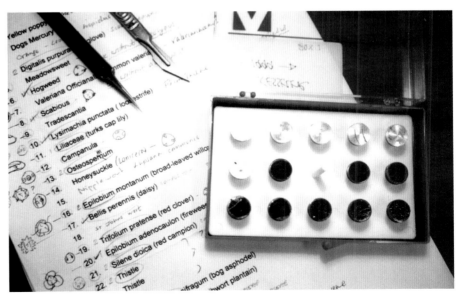

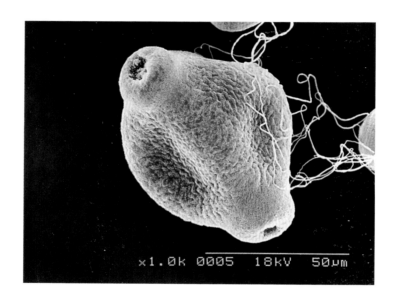

Epilobium angustifolium
Rose-bay willowherb
SEM   x1000

The literary heritage of The Lake District makes
much of the landscape, its people and its flora and fauna.
Dorothy Wordsworth's journals are full of references and
descriptions of flowers and their habitats, many of which
became immortalised in Williams poems. Similarly,
John Ruskin was fascinated by flowers and plant forms.
He drew and painted them and analysed their structures
in an attempt to find a divine order that could subsequently
be applied to painting, architecture and the applied arts.
Original manuscripts of Ruskin and Dorothy Wordsworth in
which flowers are described were photographed and the
texts enlarged, magnified. In the case of Ruskin they were
used to accompany the pollen images on the dinner service,
becoming small titles to each plate and bowl, and harking
back to the autographed souvenir cups of Brantwood that
Ruskin had made in 1887. For Dorothy her journal for the
15th of April 1802 in which she describes the celebrated
daffodils is enlarged and printed onto a tablecloth. It
becomes a backdrop to a pollen decorated tea set, the words
stained into the cloth like ghosts, traces of conversations
with her brother and the many visitors to Dove cottage.

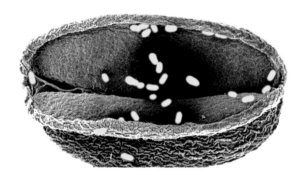

LANDSCAPING

The plantain was eight yards from me, and the scabious seven: and to my sight, at these distances, the plantain and the far-away pines were equally clear. The pines, being four miles off, showed their branches, but I could not count them: and two or three young and old Spanish chestnuts beside them showed their broken masses, only I knew the trees to be chestnuts by their general look. The plantain and the scabious in like manner I knew to be plantain and scabious by their general look.
I saw the plantain seed-vessel to be, somehow rough, and that there were two little projections at the bottom of the scabious head which I knew to mean the leaves of the calyx: but I could no more count distinctly the seeds of the plantain, or the group of leaves forming the calyx of the scabious, than I could count the branches of the far-away pines.

Under these circumstances, it is quite evident that neither the pine nor plantain could have been rightly represented by a single dot or stroke of colour. Still less could they be represented by a definite drawing, on a small scale, of a pine with all its branches clear, or of a plantain with all its seeds clear. The round dot would represent nothing, and the clear delineation too much.

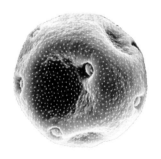

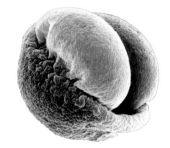

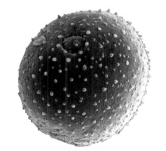

John Ruskin, Seeing Clearly,
from Modern Painters vol. IV

Daisy on front lawn at Brantwood and a pollen grain from the same flower, magnified X3,000.

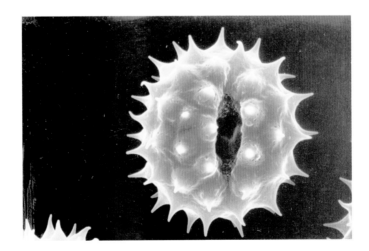

John Ruskin, Page from the original
manuscript of Proserpina, 1879.
The Ruskin Foundation (Ruskin Library,
University of Lancaster).

PROSERPINA

STUDIES OF WAYSIDE FLOWERS

WHILE THE AIR WAS YET PURE

AMONG THE ALPS, AND IN THE SCOTLAND AND ENGLAND
WHICH MY FATHER KNEW

BY

JOHN RUSKIN, LL.D.,
HONORARY STUDENT OF CHRIST CHURCH, AND SLADE PROFESSOR OF FINE ART.

VOLUME I.

1879

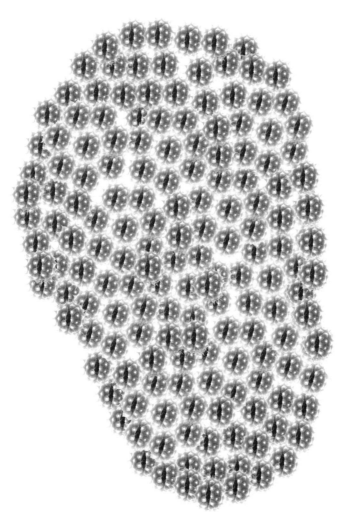

to cover the dot from the i of daisy from Ruskin's manuscript of Proserpina.

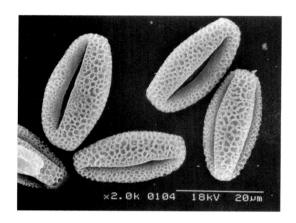

Salix caprea
Pussy willow
SEM x 2000

THE TWO BASES OF ART

I have here in my hand one of the simplest possible
examples of the union of the graphic and constructive
powers, - one of my breakfast plates . Since all the finely
architectural arts, we said, began in the shaping of the cup
and the platter, we will begin, ourselves, with the platter.

Why has it been made round? For two structural reasons:
first that the greatest holding surface may be gathered
into the smallest space: and secondly, that in being
pushed past other things on the table' it may come into
least contact with them.

Next, why has it a rim? For two other structural reasons:
first, that it is convenient to put salt or mustard upon: but
secondly and chiefly, that the plate may be easily laid hold
of. The rim is the simplest form of continuous handle.

Farther, to keep it from soiling the cloth, it will be wise to
put this ridge beneath, round the bottom: far as the rim is the
simplest form of continuous handle, so this is the simplest
form of continuous leg. And we get the section given beneath
the figure for the essential one of a rightly made platter.

Thus far our art has been strictly utilitarian, having respect
to conditions of collision, of carriage and of support. But now,
on the surface of our piece of pottery, here are various bands
and spots of colour which are presumably set there to make
it pleasanter to the eye. Six of the spots, seen closely, you
discover are intended to represent flowers. These then have a
distinctly graphic purpose as the other properties of the plate
have an architectural one, and the first critical question we
have to ask about them is, whether they are like roses or not.

John Ruskin, Aratra Pentelici, Lecture 1 1872.

It is a common flower.

John Ruskin, pressed flower, Flora of
Chamouni, 1844. Ruskin Foundation
(Ruskin Library, University of Lancaster)

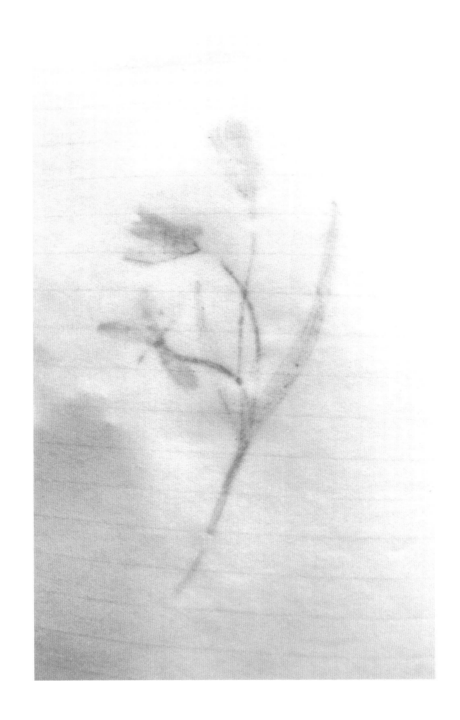

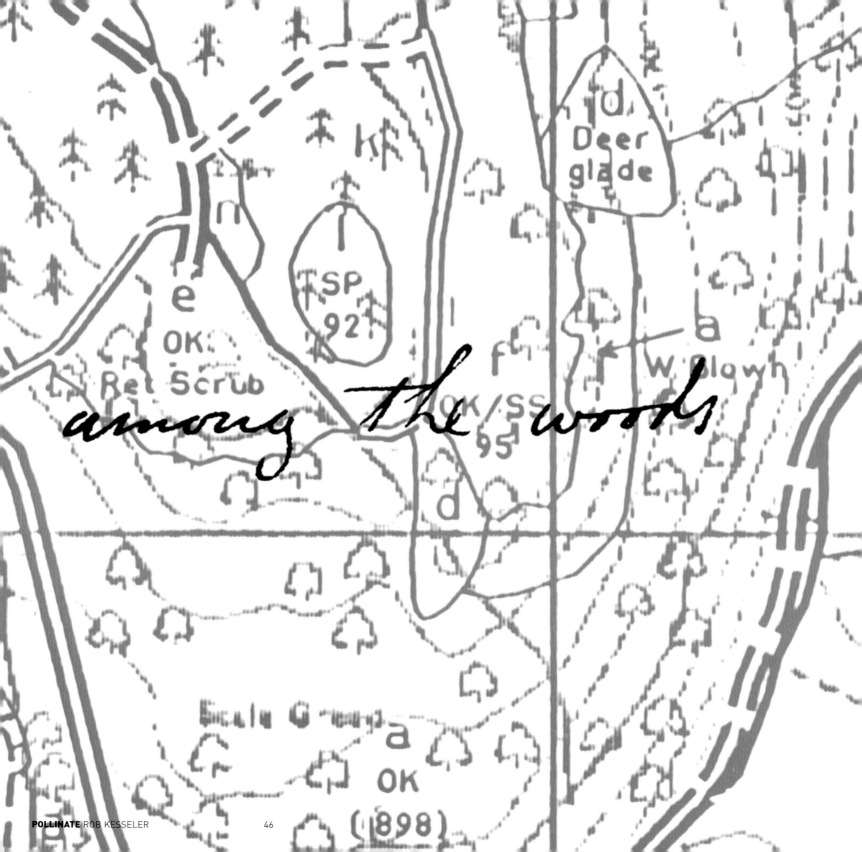

among the woods

John Ruskin, drawing of violet.
The Ruskin Foundation,
(Ruskin Library, University of Lancaster).

 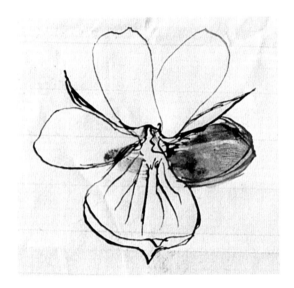

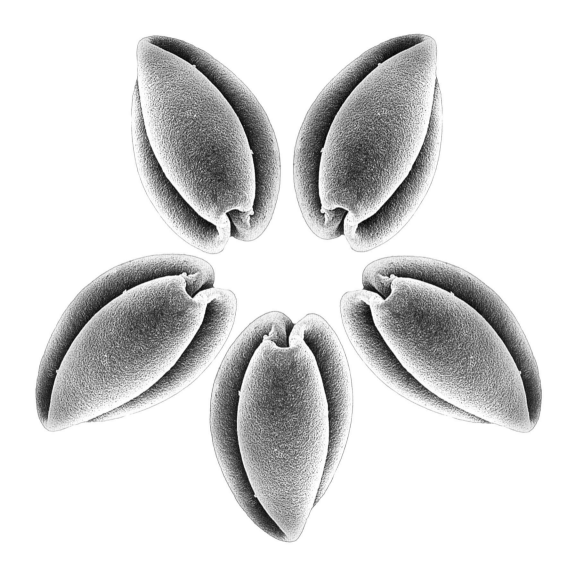

gathered

MAGIC AT LAWSON PARK

There is a moment in The Tempest that I have never seen convincingly staged. As the directions give it: "Enter Prospero above, invisible. Enter several strange shapes, bringing in a banquet; they dance about it with gentle actions of salutation; and, inviting the King, etc. to eat, they depart." Never seen convincingly staged, that is, until I was asked to dine at Lawson Park.

Meals are rituals. Magic requires ceremony. The central rite of Christianity is the breaking of bread and the drinking of wine. The wedding breakfast, the business lunch, the graduation dinner, the bump supper, the midnight feast, are rites of passage. The more formal the occasion, the greater the distance between the participants as hungry humans, takers of food and drink, and as actors, makers of a performance. At formal events we are ourselves, and something not ourselves. Ceremonies have masters, visible or invisible, commanding the strange shapes that bring in a banquet with gentle actions of salutation.

Rob Kesseler was our Prospero. A man of mystery to me, until then invisible, for I knew nothing about him and had never seen his work. But it was apparent from his invitation that the guests would be taking part as something more than themselves. Our ritual number, twelve, included a herbalist, a bee keeper, a gardener, an expert on pollen and a designer of banquets. If Robert and Pamela Woof from Dove Cottage were somehow William and Dorothy Wordsworth, then my strange shape must be intended for Ruskin's.

Not a space willingly occupied. I first saw Lawson Park in 1969 when I spent a cold, late-winter week at a conference on Ruskin in neighbouring Brantwood, sleeping in one of the rooms for the maids. It was the true start of my studies, the beginning of my professional life. For three decades I kept a proper professional distance. Yet in the year of the centenary of Ruskin1s death I had followed him to Oxford to become, like him, Slade Professor, and lecturing, like him, at the Oxford Museum. In January 2000 we had been to Coniston Church to echo the ceremonies of his funeral a hundred years before. Now, in September, I was staying once more at Brantwood, my daughters sleeping in the room where Ruskin died.

Such were the resonances that sounded as I walked up the grassy track from Brantwood to Lawson Park in clear, September summer evening light. Ahead of me, Dorothy and William Wordsworth, in gentle intimacy, were on one of their Lake District journeys. Ruskin often went this way. In the course of my walk, I went into a shepherd-farmer's cottage, to wish whoever might be in the house a happy new year. His wife was at home, of course; and his little daughter, Agnes, nine years old; both as good as gold, in their way. The cottage is nearly a model of those which I shall expect the tenants of St George's Company, and its active members, to live in; - the entire building, parlour, and kitchen (in this case one, but not necessarily so) bedrooms and all, about the size of an average dining-room, in Grosvenor Place or Park Lane.

Lawson Park in January 1875, not September 2000. Then, it was home to the Stalkers, poor tenant farmers on the land that marches with the Brantwood estate, and is now part of Grizedale forest. The director of the Grizedale Sculpture Park, Adam Sutherland, uses it as his summer dacha. Ruskin's Agnes was the youngest of eleven children. In 1875 she was another surrogate for the lost child Rose La Touche, who at the beginning of the year had been taken back to Ireland to die. Ruskin's discussion of little Agnes1s reading-matter in the February issue of Fors Clavigera, which describes his New Year visit, is a covert allusion to Rose's sickness. "Being very fond of pretty little girls (not, by any means, excluding pretty - tall ones), I choose, for my own reading, a pamphlet which has a picture of a beautiful little girl with long hair, lying very ill in bed, with her mother putting up her forefinger at her brother, who is crying, with a large tear on the side of his nose; and a legend beneath: "Harry told his mother the whole story." The pamphlet has been doubled up by Agnes right through the middle of the beautiful little girl1s face, and no less remorselessly through the very middle of the body of the "Duckling Astray", charmingly drawn by Mr Harrison Weir on the opposite leaf. But my little Agnes knows so much more about real ducklings than the artist does, that her severity in this case is not to be wondered at."

Ruskin infolds his private tragedy into Agnes's creased copy of The Children's Prize, as I interleave my story with his. The Stalkers left Lawson Park in 1883, after their mother died, moving up the valley to How Head Farm. Agnes's sister Isabella went into service at Brantwood - was it her room I had slept in?
In 1878 another sister, Hannah, became the Brantwood cook. On an earlier hill walk in 1873 Ruskin had called at Lawson Park and admired Mrs Stalker's baking: "A large pot hung over the hearth well covered with thoroughly hot turf, held six or eight small loaves side by side at the bottom. On the flat lid of the pot were loaded two inches more of hot turf. The bread was baked in an hour, Mrs Stalker said - and I never saw anything that looked nicer."

The cooking arrangements have changed at Lawson Park, and Agnes's ducklings are gone. In front of the long, low house and barn a Swiss meadow dips down towards the lake far below. There, on a wooden platform, two tables were arranged like open arms to embrace the view of the southern half of Coniston Water and Torver beyond. The bulk of the Old Man of Coniston loomed to the right, the sun lowering to the left. At our designated places, the chosen twelve found the dinner service we were there to inaugurate. Each plate bore an enlarged gilt and coloured image of a pollen sample taken from the landscape in which we sat. Each plate also bore, in Ruskin's familiar, urgent script, a fragment reproduced from the manuscript of his botanical study, Proserpina. The pine trees of Brantwood - I read from successive plates - "always on a steep slope" ... "towards the sun"... "on a bank"... had contributed the green and gold nuts of pollen on the place-setting in front of me. The napkin, specially made for this occasion, bore a sketch of a pine-cone in flower.

Was it an accident that the invitation had misprinted Proserpina as "Prosperino"? For as Kesseler came to sit at the table, the banquet appeared, brought to us by artists staying at Grizedale Park, who with gentle actions of salutation bade us eat. In The Tempest, the King of Naples and his entourage no sooner prepare to feast than with thunder and lighting Ariel appears "and, with a quaint device the table disappears." No such punishment for us. Instead a meal where everything (except the wine) came from the sunset country around us: wild mushrooms, lake chard, Grizedale venison. There were short speeches and readings, of course, from the Wordsworths and Ruskin. Tapers were brought, and as the light sank, the ritual was complete.

There is no formal ending to this narrative. Rituals exist in repetition; this rite was unique. Yet it must continue somewhere, in circular, centennial time. In the morning the weather broke, and in mist and rain my daughter Vita and I set out on our own annual ritual, a pilgrimage to the top of the Old Man.

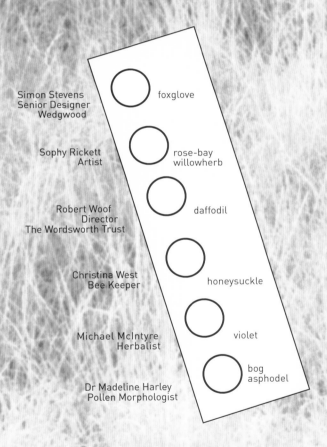

Simon Stevens
Senior Designer
Wedgwood — foxglove

Sophy Rickett
Artist — rose-bay willowherb

Robert Woof
Director
The Wordsworth Trust — daffodil

Christina West
Bee Keeper — honeysuckle

Michael McIntyre
Herbalist — violet

Dr Madeline Harley
Pollen Morphologist — bog asphodel

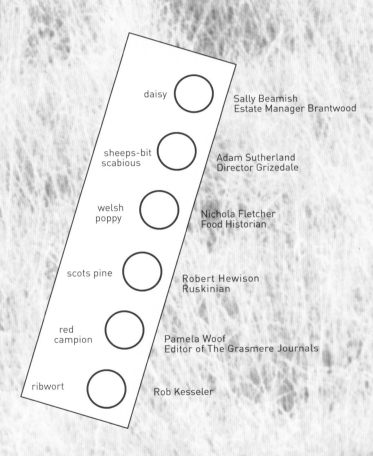

daisy — Sally Beamish
Estate Manager Brantwood

sheeps-bit scabious — Adam Sutherland
Director Grizedale

welsh poppy — Nichola Fletcher
Food Historian

scots pine — Robert Hewison
Ruskinian

red campion — Pamela Woof
Editor of The Grasmere Journals

ribwort — Rob Kesseler

THE PARTICIPANTS

MENU DEVISED BY NICHOLA FLETCHER

MEAL PREPARED AND SERVED BY
KIM WALSH, AGALIS MANESSI AND CLAIRE TODD

PHOTOGRAPHY BY CLAIRE SHOOSMITH AND JENNY BROWNRIGG

HONEY FROM CHRISTINA WEST, YEWFIELD

HERBAL MOSQUITO REPELLENT BY MICHAEL MCINTYRE

FUNGHI TABLE DECORATIONS BY ADAM SUTHERLAND

RUSKIN READING BY ROBERT HEWISON

WORDSWORTH READINGS BY ROBERT AND PAMELA WOOF

APPLES FROM RUSKIN'S GARDEN BY SALLY BEAMISH

CHINA FROM WEDGWOOD BY SIMON STEVENS

POLLEN PREPARATION BY DR. MADELINE HARLEY

FOREST FRUITS BY SOPHY RICKETT

A RUSKIN READING

Ruskin's introduction to his notes on the set of teaching examples he had created for use by his students in what was to become the Ruskin Drawing School at Oxford. The notes are addressed to the Slade Professor's privileged students, in order to remind them of the moral and social obligations of art.

They were written in his London home, no 163 Denmark Hill, Camberwell.

I went into my garden at half past six on the morning of April 21, 1870, to think over the final order of these examples for you.

The air was perfectly calm, the sunlight pure, and falling on the grass through thickets of the standard peach (which had blossomed that year perfectly), and of plum and pear trees, in their first showers of fresh silver, looking more like much- broken and far-tossed spray of fountains than trees: and just at the end of my hawthorn walk, one happy nightingale was as much as he could in every moment.

Meantime, in the still air, the roar of the railroads from Clapham Junction, New Cross, and the Crystal Palace (I am between the three), sounded constantly and heavily, like the surf of a strong sea three or four miles distant: and the whistles of the trains passing nearer mixed with the nightingale's notes. That I could hear at all, or see the blossoms, or the grass, in the best time of spring, depended

on my having been long able to spend a large sum annually in self-indulgence, and in keeping my fellow-creatures out of my way.

Of those who were causing all that murmur, like the sea, round me, and the myriads imprisoned by the English Minotaur of lust for wealth, and condemned to live, if it is to be called life, in the labyrinth of black walls, and loathsome passages between them, which now fills the valley of the Thames, and is called London, not one could hear, that day, any happy bird sing, or look upon any quiet space of the pure grass that is good for seed.

But they might have the blessing of these things for all and each of them, if they chose, and that vast space of London might be full of gardens, and terraced round with hawthorn walks, with children at play in them, as fair as their blossoms.

And now gentlemen, I beg you once for all to understand that unless you are minded to bring yourselves, and all whom you can help, out of this curse of darkness that has fallen on our hearts and thoughts, you need not try to do any art-work, - it is the vainest of affections to try to put beauty into shadows, while all the real things that cast them are in deformity and pain.

The Works of John Ruskin (Library Edition) Vol.211,pp 103-4, Catalogue of the Educational Series, 1871.

Read by Robert Hewison.

MENU FOR A FOREST FEAST

○

Selection of bread with green herb sauce
Platter of appetisers

○

Marinated wood pigeon
Caramelised shallots
Salad leaves and herbs
Tiny toasts with grilled local cheese and wild garlic
Marinated trout
Beetroot
Horseradish
Seasonal vegetables with mustard dressing

○

Wild mushroom soup

○

Grilled arctic char with rowan jelly sauce

○

Grilled Grizedale venison (red & sika deer)
with a honey roasted damson sauce
Carrot puree
Potatoes savoyarde
Roast peppers
Sliced aubergine salad

○

Local cream cheese served with a compote of forest fruits
and cumberland ginger Biscuits

○

Coffee served with violet, rose and honey pine pastilles

"There are not many places in the world where one can go out of the woods into a space domed by a variegated sky striated to the west - the land, the water, the black mountain and the various hues from blue to grey and diminishing crimsons: all that before the articulating stars ('so geometrical that something could be proved'); and there the postulating companions finding the moving satellite, wandering at a fast walking pace along the other apparently fixed stars."

Robert Woof
Extract of letter to Rob Kesseler after the Dinner

Fair seed -time had my soul, and I grew up
Fostered alike by beauty and by fear;
Much favored in my birthplace, and no less
In that beloved Vale to which, erelong,
I was transplanted. Well I call to mind
('Twas at an early age,ere I had seen
Nine summers) when upon the mountain slope
The frost and breath of frosty wind had snapped
The last autumnal crocus, 'twas my joy
To wander half the night among the Cliffs
And the smooth Hollows, where the woodcocks ran
Along the open turf. In thought and wish
That time, my shoulder all with springes hung,
I was a fell destroyer. On the heights
Scudding away from snare to snare, I plied
My anxious visitation, hurrying on,
Still hurrying, hurrying onward: moon and stars
Were shining o'er my head: I was alone,
And seemed to be a trouble to the peace
That was among them. Sometimes it befel
In these night-wanderings, that a strong desire
O'erpowered my better reason, and the bird
Which was the captive of anothers toils
Became my prey: and, when the deed was done
I heard among the hills
Low breathings coming after me, and sounds
Of indistinguishable motion, steps
Almost as silent as the turf they trod.

Nor less in springtime when on southern banks
The shining sun had from his knot of leaves
Decoyed the primrose flower, and when the Vales
And woods were warm, was I a plunderer then
In the high places, on the lonesome peaks
Where'er among the mountains and the winds,
The Mother Bird had built her lodge. Though mean
My object, and inglorious, yet the end
Was not ignoble, Oh! when I have hung
Above the raven's nest, by knots of grass
And half-inch fissures in the slippery rock
But ill sustained, and almost, as it seemed,
Suspended by the blast which blew amain,
Shouldering the naked crag: Oh! at that time,
While on the perilous ridge I hung alone,
With what strange utterance did the loud dry wind
Blow through my ears! the sky seemed not a sky
Of earth, and with what motion moved the clouds!

The Prelude Book 1
William Wordsworth
Read by Robert Woof

on gathering a flower

TEA AND THE WORDSWORTHS

Painter, put as many books as you can into the room. Make it populous with books; and furthermore, paint me a good fire; and furniture plain and modest... And near the fire paint me a tea-table... place only two cups and saucers on the tea-tray; and, if you know how to paint such a thing, symbolically or otherwise, paint me an eternal tea-pot...

This room with the books is the upstairs sitting-room at Dove Cottage, Town End, Grasmere, home of Wordsworth and his sister Dorothy from Christmas 1799, and of his wife Mary Hutchinson from October 1802. The three of them – and three children – were there until May 1808. The tea-table described could have been Wordsworth's, but it is not; it is that of the next tenant of the cottage, De Quincey, who moved in, in 1809. The 'eternal tea-pot' would have betrayed this, for De Quincey goes on to remark, 'I usually drink tea from eight o'clock at night to four in the morning.' Wordsworth was not so continuous a drinker; tea would be drunk on most days at Dove Cottage – Dorothy mentions it frequently in her Journal, but in Wordsworth's time tea seemed to punctuate the late afternoon or early evening hours rather than occupy the greater part of the night. Further,

another receptacle was generally on De Quincey's tea-table: a glass 'sublunary wine-decanter'. Into this, continued De Quincey, 'you may put a quart of ruby-coloured laudanum'. While De Quincey prolonged his ritual of tea-drinking and opium drops into the small hours and into solitude the Wordsworths in the same room were sociable as they drank tea at some point between dinner, at about three o'clock, and something to eat before bed – supper. Nothing was fixed however; no hours were rigid. The Wordsworths were at ease, and at home.

Their very coming to the North-West was a kind of coming home, although when Wordsworth and his sister arrived at Dove Cottage they came to an empty house in a valley that Wordsworth had been in briefly some two or three times, and Dorothy, once. Wordsworth was 29 and Dorothy almost 28. They had never before had to furnish a house, make a garden or get to know a valley and its people. In May 1800 Wordsworth and their brother John set off into Yorkshire to see the Hutchinsons, and Dorothy began a Journal which lasted not only for the three weeks of her brothers' absence but for three years. Alone, she would still take tea between dinner and supper.

16 May 1800: After dinner Aggy [a neighbour] weeded onions & carrots – I helped for a little – wrote to Mary Hutchinson – washed my head – worked. After tea went to Ambleside... No letters!... Grasmere was very solemn in the last glimpse of twilight it calls home the heart to quietness... I finished my letter to MH. – ate hasty pudding, & went to bed.

Besides walking to Ambleside and back after tea, Dorothy that day had transplanted radishes, gathered 'some wild plants' and walked round Grasmere lake. She would need the hasty pudding she had for supper – oatmeal (or sometimes flour) stirred into boiling milk or milk and water, a kind of porridge. Three or four times while Wordsworth and John were away, her taking tea, as on this day in the early evening, was prelude to a new activity, such as walking the four miles to Ambleside for the post.

But tea-time was a time for talking, frequently with visitors. On several occasions during Wordsworth's absence the Simpsons called on Dorothy, walking into Grasmere from their house up the Raise, taking Dorothy a further long walk, gathering broom, getting strawberries, fishing, and returning to drink tea at Town End:

'Mr, Miss Simpson & Tommy drank tea at 8 o'clock – I walked to the Potters with them' (31 May 1800). A week later, grandson Tommy came alone, and needed more than tea; Dorothy had 'walked up to Mr Simpsons to gather gooseberries – it was a very fine afternoon – little Tommy came down with me, ate gooseberries & drank tea with me'. Both of them then took up plants for the garden from the hill-side and from the lake-shore. That night, Wordsworth returned from Yorkshire after 11 o'clock, and 'after our first joy was over we got some tea'. Tea was refreshment after a journey as well as a social ritual.

Tea was taken with the Simpsons right through the Journal, sometimes followed by a round of cards. Old Mr Simpson and his two daughters called, for instance, on 13 November 1800, 'found us at dinner'. They all then, 'drank tea & supped played at cards.' This was the Wordsworths' third successive evening of tea that led on to supper; Dorothy began to have headaches, and twice that week had to send to the Lloyds to excuse herself from similar evenings. Tea could be associated with an over-hectic social life.

Food was taken at supper, and this was not always hasty pudding or the bread and butter that Dorothy carried to Wordsworth when he 'came in sleepy, & hurried to bed' on 14 June 1802. On 2 December 1800, for instance, Priscilla Lloyd 'drank tea with us', and then they all walked to Ambleside and 'Supped upon a hare'. And once, having drunk 'tea at a farmhouse' in Wythburn, Coleridge and the Wordsworths walked back to Dove Cottage and they had mutton chops and potatoes for supper.

The Wordsworths got to know their neighbours through the ritual of tea-drinking. They drank tea not only with the Simpson family, and the Lloyds of Brathay, but with Mr and Mrs Olliff who had built the Hollins, a new 'trim box' in Dorothy's words on the fell-side not far from Town End. Mr Clarkson from Ullswater came in to tea, Mr Luff from Ambleside and Patterdale, and, from more distant parts, Jones and Mr Palmer, Mr Marshall, and Mr Twining, the great London tea-dealer and future supplier of tea to the Wordsworths. Dorothy uses the title 'Mr', even in her Journal, to denote the educated and the gentleman, sometimes dropping it familiarly as in the case of Robert Jones, Wordsworth's old Cambridge travelling companion, Charles Lloyd, or Stoddart whom Wordsworth had known in his early London republican days. All these persons had tea at Dove Cottage.

The Wordsworths' humbler neighbours tended to ask them to tea; they drank tea at Betty Dixon's, John Fisher's, and Frank Baty's. Molly Fisher, the old woman who did the vegetables, the fires and the washing for Dorothy, is recorded once as going out to tea, and young Sally Ashburner opposite visited at Mr Simpson's. Tea-drinking was a habit in all ranks of society in Grasmere valley. Occasionally it was an addiction. When Betty Towers and her little son and daughter came to tea, Betty Towers told Dorothy that she and her husband were 'so tender in their health that they must be obliged to sell their Land' (21 June 1802), and in connection with such economic hardship she recounted the case of old Jim Jackson who had begun 'with a clear Estate'. 'How did they get through with their money?' asks Dorothy in the Journal, as though re-living the conversation. "Why in eating & drinking." The wife would make tea 4 or 5 times in a day & "sec folks for sugar!" Then she would have nea Teapot but she would take the water out of a Brass pan on the fire & pour it on to the Tea in a quart pot. This all for herself, for she boiled the tea leaves, always for her Husband & their son.'

Not 4 or 5 times, but once a day was the Wordsworths' moderate custom, and they clearly thought that tea did them good. Once, not feeling very well, Dorothy was 'inclined to go to bed when we reached home, but Wm persuaded me to have tea instead' (30 June 1802). Far from going to bed, she then wrote a lengthy Journal entry describing the life of an old man who had been servant to the Marquis of Granby, a letter to Coleridge, finished a letter to Mary Hutchinson and declared herself 'somewhat better'. Several times she records feeling 'better after tea'. Just occasionally tea was substantial; when there had been no dinner they had 'Gooseberry pie to our tea' (12 June 1802), and when Mary Hutchinson came to Grasmere as Wordsworth's wife, she and Dorothy, 'not quite well but better after tea', set to and 'made Cakes &c'. Next day, 17 October 1802, 'We had 13 of our neighbours to Tea — Wm came in just as we began tea'. It was a belated wedding feast, Wordsworth getting back from visiting Coleridge in Keswick just in time.

Yet it was the ordinary everyday tea that Wordsworth, it would appear, liked best; less the tea with visitors, than the quiet anticipation of tea in the peaceful house:

I am not One who much or oft delight
To season my fireside with personal talk About Friends who live within an easy walk, Or Neighbours, daily, weekly, in my sight... Better than such discourse doth silence long,Long, barren silence, square with my desire; To sit without emotion, hope, or aim, By my half-kitchen my half-parlour fire, And listen to the flapping of the flame, Or kettle, whispering its faint undersong. ('Personal Talk')

Once, Wordsworth escaped from Miss Simpson when she called, and sat in his own room until she went (11 February 1802). He had to balance social life with his need for calm, a calm that had not even the energy of meditation, no pensive component, but rather the vacant mood of listening only to the fire's sounds or the faint undersong of the kettle on the hob as it stood in readiness for the making of tea. The half-kitchen, half-parlour fire of the

sonnet was probably that in the main room downstairs. The Wordsworths could make tea upstairs or down, and could, in the upstairs parlour manage toast at the fire, perhaps for a simple supper, sitting 'both at the little green round table by the fireside, the watch ticking above our heads' (Dorothy to Coleridge, 6 March 1804).

With the birth of children, quietness in the house was harder to find and it became important to have a more removed place to drink tea in out of doors on fine days. Tea outside was rare. Dorothy, in Langdale valley all day, as Wordsworth fished in Elterwater, 'was much tired' on 23 June 1800, '& returned home to tea', while 'W went to fish for pike in Rydale. John came in when I had done tea, & he & I carried a jug of tea to William. We met him in the old road from Rydale – he drank his tea upon the turf.' The tea would be still just warm in its jug. Only on special occasions was a fire lit and a kettle boiled out of doors. The Coleridge family stayed at Dove Cottage for three and a half weeks in July 1800 on their way to Greta Hall, Keswick, where they were to live. Two high points of their stay were tea-drinkings, one on Grasmere island and the other on the wooded shore of the lake; both are mentioned in Dorothy's scant summary:

On the Friday preceding their departure we drank tea at the island. The weather very delightful - & on the Sunday we made a great fire, & drank tea in Bainriggs with the Simpsons – it was

excessively hot – Coleridge made a mystical moment of this when he wrote to Humphry Davy on 25 July:

We drank tea the night before I left Grasmere on the Island in that lovely lake, our kettle swung over the fire hanging from the branch of a Fir Tree, and I lay & saw the woods & mountains, & lake all trembling, & as it were idealised thro' the subtle smoke which rose up from the clear red embers of the fir-apples which we had collected. Afterwards we made a glorious Bonfire on the Margin, by some alder bushes, whose twigs heaved & sobbed in the uprushing column of smoke - & the Image of the Bonfire, & of us that danced round it – ruddy laughing faces in the twilight...

Grand as these tea-drinkings were, the Wordsworths simply wanted a place removed from the flurry of the house which was yet close enough for tea to be carried out and drunk hot. A door, through the kindness of the Clarksons, was made in 1804 in the wall at the back of the house at the turning of the staircase. Its upper half was glass and for the first time the Wordsworths were able to go directly from the house to the garden, and to look out continually into the orchard. More than that. 'We have been busily employed', wrote Dorothy on 25 December to Lady Beaumont, 'about finishing a little hut or shed, a sort of larger Bird's nest (for it is lined with moss) at the top of our Orchard, a place for my Brother to retire to for quietness on warm days in winter and for a pleasure-house, a little parlour for all of us in the summer – it is large enough for a large party to drink tea in.' But the little shed remained unfinished for a time. John Wordsworth's death when his ship went down off Weymouth Bay in February 1805 meant, said Dorothy, that 'we durst not look in the face of anything we loved... For three months I was only once on the top of the Orchard.' But they did 'summon up' their hearts and by 8 June 1805 they were spending, wrote Dorothy, 'many sweet hours', some of them tea-drinking hours, in the moss hut. Tea was expensive. But John Wordsworth in the course of his voyages with the East India Company was able to buy in China, and indeed he invested money and made a profit on tea (though a balancing loss on woollen goods) as the price of tea rose in England. In 1803 he was sending a Box of Tea up to Grasmere. After John's death the Wordsworths bought from Mr Richard Twining – who had called at Dove Cottage in August 1800 and with whom John hoped to establish a business connection. Dorothy's letters concerning payments to Mr Twining indicate sums of between fourteen and sixteen pounds per year. A typical order of 1813 was for '40lb of Souchong tea at 7/- 1lb Pekoe Tea – and 1lb of the best black tea'. The tea would be put on the Kendal wagon in London; later, after 1819, it would be transported by canal to Lancaster, and then to Kendal. The Wordsworths' own used tea leaves were dried and given away. We do not know what kind of tea pot or tea cups the family had in the Dove Cottage days. It is certain that Dorothy had tea cups because she was prepared to follow Lady Beaumont's advice and 'put a tea cup full of sweet Oil into the Cask' of brown Stout when first tapping the cask. This particular cask had been a gift from the Beaumonts, not yet tapped because the Wordsworths were still finishing the last cask of their own ale (29 May 1804). Their drink with meals would be ale, water, or occasionally wine. Tea was itself, drunk and enjoyed for itself. Undoubtedly China cups were used for the delicate China tea. Two such charming Wordsworth cups and saucers exist from the more prosperous Rydal Mount years. Their pretty colours and flowered designs are on view in the Wordsworth Museum, and as the Journal nears its end, one can imagine the sweet domestic scene as Dorothy Wordsworth calmly celebrates her thirty-first birthday, late on Christmas Eve 1802. The time of course is after tea:

William is now sitting by me at _ past 10 o'clock. I have been beside him ever since tea running the heel of a stocking, repeating some of his sonnets to him, listening to his own repeating, reading some of Milton's & the Allegro & Penseroso... Mary is well & I am well, & Molly is as blithe as last year at this time.

In winter by the fire, in warmer weather sitting on the terrace wall, or in the moss hut, encircled not only by the hills but by the many plants and flowers that had been collected from the fells and the lake shore, the Wordsworths drank tea, and that act in itself was a part of the creative and rich pattern of their lives.

PAMELA WOOF

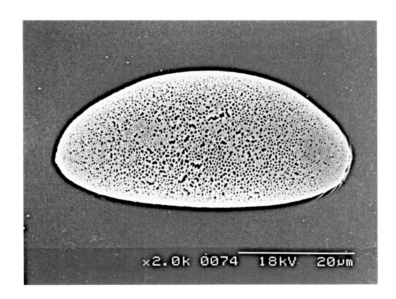

Narcissuss pseudonarcissus
Daffodil
SEM x 2000

THURSDAY 15TH APRIL, 1802

It was a threatening misty morning - but mild. We set off after dinner from Eusmere - Mrs Clarkson went a short way with us but turned back. The wind was furious & we thought we must have returned. We first rested in a large Boat-house, then under a furze Bush opposite Mr. Clarksons, saw the plough going in the field. The wind seized our breath, the Lake was rough. There was a boat by itself floating in the middle of the Bay below Water Millock - We rested again in the Water Millock lane. The hawthorns are black & green, the birches here & there greenish but there is yet more of purple to be seen on the Twigs. We got over into a field to avoid some cows- people working, a few primroses by the roadside, woodsorrel flowers, the anemone, scentless violets, strawberries, & that starry yellow flower Mrs C calls pile wort. When we were in the woods beyond Gowbarrow park we saw a few daffodils close to the waterside, we fancied that the lake had floated the seeds ashore & that the little colony had so sprung up - But as we went along there were more & yet more & at last under the boughs of the trees, we saw that there was a long belt of them along the shore, about the breadth of a country turnpike road. I never saw daffodils so beautiful they grew among the mossy stones about & about them, some rested their heads upon these stones as on a pillow for weariness & the rest tossed & reeled & danced and seemed as if verily they laughed with the wind that blew upon them over the Lake. they looked so gay ever glancing ever changing. This wind blew directly over the Lake to them. There was here & there a little knot & a few stragglers a few yards higher up but they were so few as not to disturb the simplicity & unity & and life of that one busy highway - We rested again & again. The Bays were stormy & we heard the waves at different distances & in the middle of the water like the sea.

The Grasmere Jounals
Dorothy Wordsworth, Journal 15th April 1802. The Wordsworth Trust

'I never saw daffodils so
beautiful they grew among
the mossy stones about & about
them, some rested their heads
upon these stones as on a
pillow for weariness & the
rest tossed & reeled & ma
& seemed

flowers

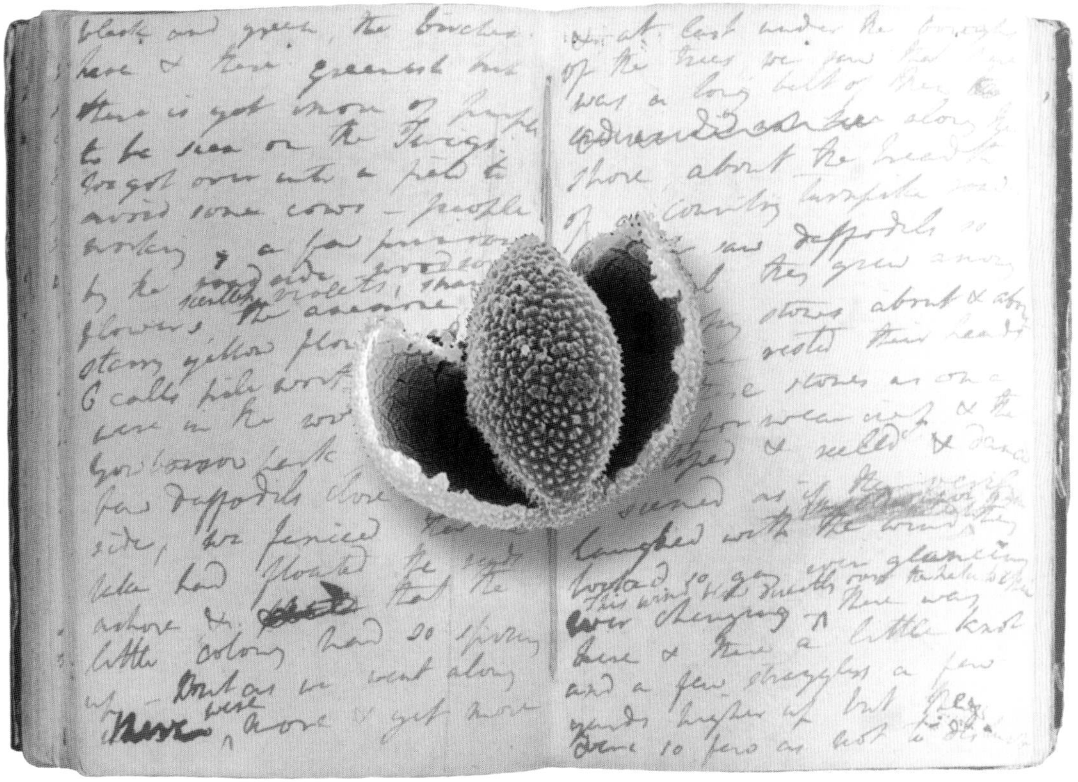

promiscuously

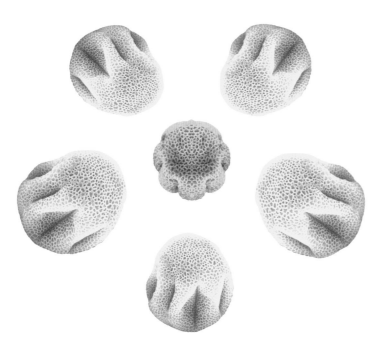

DRANK TEA

The Journals of Dorothy Wordsworth are resplendent with references to the flowers and plants she observed and collected on her walks around the lakes and over the hills near the home at Grasmere she shared with her brother William. Described in great detail and immortalised in his poems, many were brought back to create the garden at Dove Cottage. These many descriptions (well over 250) are almost equalled by as many references to drinking tea. Supped with William by the fireside, and with their various friends and acquaintances locally or passing through. The social act of drinking tea can be seen as a metaphor for cross-pollination, a fertile exchange where observations gathered each day germinate and take new form. Pollinate is a tea service specially created for Dove Cottage that brings together images of pollen collected from flowers in their garden merged with fragments of text from the Journal. A conversation piece.

SUNDAY 12TH OCTOBER 1800

We walked before tea by Brainriggs
to observe the many coloured foliage
the oaks dark green with yellow leaves
- The birches generally still green,
some near the water yellowish. The
Sycamore crimson & crimson-tufted -
the mountain ash a deep orange - the
common ash Lemon colour but many
ashes still fresh in their summer
green. Those that were discoloured
were chiefly near the water. William
composing in the evening. Went to
be at 12 o'clock.

THURSDAY 6TH MAY 1802

The Ash Trees are in blossom,
Birds flying all about us. The stitchwort
is coming out, there is one budding
Lychnis. The primroses are passing
their prime. Celandine violets &
wood sorrel for ever more - little
geranium & pansies on the wall.
We walked in the evening to Tail End
to enquire about hurdles for the
orchard shed & about Mr Luff's flower -
The flower dead - no hurdles.

WEDNESDAY 12TH MAY 1802

A sunshiny but coldish morning - we
walked into Easdale & returned by
George Rowson's & the lane. We bought
home heckberry blossom, crab
blossom - the anemone nemorosa -
Marsh Marygold - Speedwell, that
beautiful blue one the colour of the
blue stone or glass used in jewellery,
with its beautiful pearl-like chives -
anemones are in abundance & still dear
primroses violets in beds, pansies in
abundance, & the little celandine. I
pulled a branch of the taller celandine.
Butterflies of all colours _ I often see
some small ones of a pale purple lilac
or Emperor's eye colour something of
the colour of that large geranium that
grows by the lake side. Wm observed
the beauty of Geordy Green's house. We
see it from our orchard. Wm pulled ivy
with beautiful berries - I put it over the
chimney piece - sate in the orchard
the hour before dinner, coldish.
We have now dined. My head aches -
William is sleeping in the window.

FRIDAY 28TH MAY 1802

There is yet one primrose in the
orchard - the stitchwort is fading - the
wild columbines are coming into beauty
- the vetches are in abundance
Blossoming and seeding. That pretty
little waxy looking Dial-like yellow
flower, the speedwell, & some others
whose names I do not yet know.

WEDNESDAY 6TH JULY 1802

A very fine day. William had slept
ill so he lay in bed till 11o'clock.
I wrote to John, ironed the Linen,
packed up, lay in the orchard all
afternoon. In the morning Wm nailed
up the trees while I was ironing.
We lay sweetly in the Orchard the
well is beautiful the orchard full of
Foxgloves the honeysuckle beautiful -
plenty of roses but they are battered.
Wrote to Molly Ritson & Coleridge.
Walked on the White Moss - glow-
worms - well for them children
are in bed when they shine.

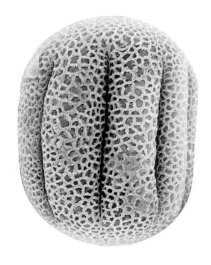

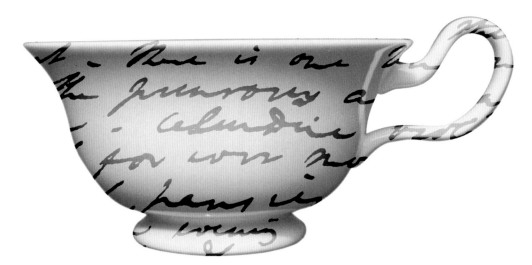

calandria

stars yellow flower

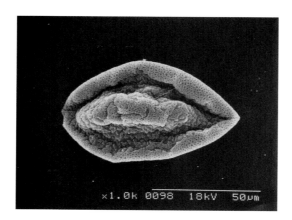

Erythronium dens-canis
Dog's tooth violet
SEM x 1000

WEDNESDAY 14TH MAY 1800

The lake looked to me I knew not
why dull and melancholy, the weltering
on the shores seemed to me a heavy
sound. I walked as long as I could
amongst the stones of the shore.
The wood rich in flowers. A beautiful
yellow, palish yellow flower, that looked
thick round & double, & smelt very
sweet - I suppose it was a ranunculus -
Crowfoot, the grassy leaved Rabbit-
toothed white flower, strawberries,
Geranium - scentless violet, anemones
two kinds, orchises, primroses.
The heckberry very beautiful as a
low shrub.

FRIDAY 16TH MAY 1800

Warm and mild after a fine night of
rain. Transplanted raddishes after
breakfast. We walked to Mr Gells with
the books - gathered mosses & plants.
The woods extremely beautiful with all
autumnal variety & softness - I carried
a basket for mosses, & gathered some
wild plants. Oh! that we had a book of
botany - all the flowers now are gay
& deliciously sweet. The primrose still
pre-eminent among the later flowers
of spring. Foxgloves very tall - with
their heads budding.

SUNDAY 22ND JUNE 1800

In the morning W & I walked
towards Rydale & up into the wood
but finding it not very pleasant we
returned _ sauntered in the garden -
a showery day. In the evening I
planted honeysuckle round the
yew tree. In the evening we walked
for letters. No letters, no news of
Coleridge. Jimmy Benson came
home drunk beside us.

WEDNESDAY 25TH JUNE 1800

A very rainy day - I made a shoe -
Wm & John went to fish in Langdale.
In the evening I went above the
house, & gathered flowers which
I planted, foxglove &c.

SUNDAY JULY 26TH 1800

After tea we rowed down to Loughrigg
Fell, visited the white foxglove, gathered
wild strawberries & walked up to view
Rydale we lay a long time looking at the
lake, the shores all embrowned with
the scorching sun. The ferns were
turning yellow, that is here & there
one was quite turned.

FRIDAY 7TH NOVEMBER 1800

A cold rainy morning Wm still unwell.
I working and reading Amelia. The
Michaelmas daisy droops. The pansies
are full of flowers. The Ashes opposite
are green, all but one but they have lost
many of their leaves. The copses are
quite brown. The poor woman & child
from Whitehaven drank tea - nothing
warm that day.

the colour

of the blue stone

we drank tea in
the orchard

TUESDAY 14TH JUNE 1800

William & I went upon the water to set pike floats - John fished under Loughrigg. We returned to dinner - 2 pikes boiled & roasted - a very cold air but warm sun. W & I again went upon the water - we walked to Rydale after tea, & up to the potter's - a cold night but warmer.

TUESDAY 24TH JUNE 1800

W went to Ambleside - John walked out - I made tarts &c - Mr B Simpson called & asked us to tea - I went to the view of Rydale to meet William. John went to meet him - I returned - W & I drank tea at Mr Simpsons, brought down Lemon Thyme, green &c - The old woman was very happy to see us & we were so in the pleasure we gave. She was an afflicting picture of Patient disappointment suffering under no particular affliction.

FRIDAY 1ST AUGUST 1800

In the morning I copied The Brothers - Coleridge & Wm went down to the lake. They returned & we all went together to Mary Point where we sate in the breeze & the shade & read Wms poems altered 'The Whirlblast & c' - Mr. Simpson came to tea & Mr. B Simpson afterwards - we drank tea in the orchard.

WEDNESDAY 10TH MARCH 1802

A fine mildish morning that is, not frost - Wm read in Ben Johnson in the morning. I read a little German altered Sara's waistcoats. We then walked to Rydale - No letters! - they are slashing away in Benson's wood - We walked round by the Church, through Olliff's field when we returned, then home & went up into the orchard. We sate on the Seat, talked a little by the fire, & then got our tea - William has since Tea been talking about publishing the Yorkshire Wolds poem with the Pedlar.

FRIDAY 25TH MARCH 1802

We did not walk though it was a fine day. Mr. Simpson drank tea with us. No letter from Coleridge.

SUNDAY MORNING 9TH MAY 1802

The air considerably colder today but the sun shone all day - William worked at the Leech gatherer almost incessantly from morning till tea-time. I copied the Leech-gatherer & other poems for Coleridge - I was oppressed & sick at heart for he wearied himself to death. After tea he wrote 2 stanzas in the manner of Thomsons Castle of Indolence - & was tired out. Bad news of Coleridge.

TUESDAY 19TH AUGUST 1800
Mr. Simpson dined with us - Miss S
& Brother drank tea in the orchard.

Monday 24th November 1800
A fine morning. Sara & I walked to
Rydale. After dinner we went to the
Lloyds & drank tea & supped - a
sharp cold night with sleet and
snow. I had tooth-ache in the night -
took Laudanum.

THURSDAY 12TH NOVEMBER 1801
A beautiful sunshiny day. We rose very
late. I put the rag Boxes in order.
We walked out while the goose was
roasting - we walked to the top of the
Hill. M & I followed Wm as walking
upon the Turf between John's Grove
& the Lane - it was a most sweet noon
- we did not go into John's Grove but we
walked among the Rocks & there we
sate. Mr. Olliff passed Mary & me upon
the Road Wm still among the Rocks.
The Lake beautiful from the Orchard.
Wm & I walked out before tea - The
Crescent moon - we sate in the Slate
quarry I sate there a long time alone.
Wm reached home before me - I found
them at Tea. There were a thousand
stars in the Sky.

FRIDAY11TH DECEMBER 1801
Baked pies & cakes. It was a stormy
morning with Hail showers. The Luffs
dined with us - Mrs l came with Mrs
Olliff in the Gig. We sate lazily round the
fire after dinner. Mr. & mrs Olliff drank
tea and supped with us - a hard frost
when they came.

THURSDAY 22ND NOVEMBER 1801
Breakfasted at Penny Bridge dined
at Conniston - a grand stormy day -
drank tea at home.

WEDNESDAY 9TH JUNE 1802
Wm slept ill. A soaking all-day Rain.
We should have gone to Mr. Simpson's
to tea but we walked up after tea.
Lloyds called. The Hawthorns on the
mountain sides like orchards in
blossom. Brought Rhubarb down.
It rained hard. Ambleside Fair.

SATURDAY 16TH OCTOBER 1802
Came home Mary & I, William returned
to Coleridge before we reached Nadel
Fell. Mary & I had a pleasant walk, the
day was very bright, the people busy
getting in their corn - reached home at
about 5 o clock. I was not quite well but
better after tea, we made cakes &c -

SUNDAY 17TH OCTOBER 1802
We had 13 of our neighbours to Tea -
Wm came in just as tea began.

TUESDAY 19TH OCTOBER 1802
The Simpsons drank tea and supped.
William was much oppressed.

the brooks — the lake

I walked out before
scent moon — we
the State quarry
a long time a

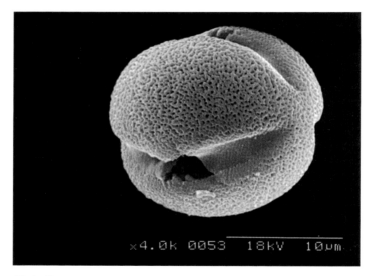

Digitalis purpurea
Foxglove
SEM x4000